MW01012044

GROWING OLD
UNGRACEFULLY

PHIL KLINE

Growing Old Ungracefully

Copyright © 2014 Phil Kline

ISBN – 13: 978-1502967282
ISBN – 10: 1502967286

PRINTED IN THE USA

ONE

ALTERNATIVES

In a Dale Carnegie course, Otto, a doctor, gave a talk stating that people should have a living will to prevent others from keeping them alive, which some doctors and family members want for them. He said, "Most older people would rather die with dignity as an alternative to spending the rest of their time on earth as a vegetable." I made the decision that night to die with dignity, when it was my time to go, rather than live as a vegetable. I decided to make a living will.

At age forty-three, a year after hearing Otto's talk, I developed pains in my stomach. I went to see my doctor, Hugo, and he sent me to a specialist in gastroenterology. After sticking a tube down my throat and taking a photo of my stomach, this specialist in stomach disorders diagnosed my problem as inoperable cancer. He said an operation was out of the question, but I could undergo chemotherapy, which at that time, may have prolonged my life for six months or a year. I decided the best thing to protect my wife, two teen sons, and five-year-old daughter from trauma, was not to undergo chemo that would only keep me alive for a while. I checked my life insurance to make sure my beneficiaries were up to date, made sure my will was current, and made a living will. I told my wife what I'd done, and she agreed it was my decision to make.

Eleven days from the date I was told I had stomach cancer, Hugo called and said, "The gastroenterologist made a mistake. You don't have cancer."

"How do you know?" I asked.

"Pathology. You have a disease I can't pronounce, so I call it gonorrhea of the stomach."

I was saved after having been classified as terminal by a specialist in stomach disorders, who had never heard of Menetriers Disease, the name Peruvian-born Hugo could not pronounce.

My Menetriers has been in remission for forty years, leaving me as a person who made the decision to die with dignity and lived to tell about it. Because of what I've been through, and because of my aging, I'm able to write about how I've handled growing old, and I can help you understand what the future has in store just waiting to grab you.

My daughter now has a grown-up daughter of her own, Ashley, who is a navy hospital corpsman, doing rehab for Marines. When Ashley was home on leave two years ago, I mentioned that I was getting old. She turned toward me and said, "You're not getting old, Grampa, you are old." That comment didn't cause a problem other than to bruise my ego. But it helped make me see life as a one-way street on which I didn't want to be headed the wrong way.

Nobody had called me old before Ashley said it. As a child, I assumed old people had been born that way. At least, I had never given it much thought. Until the age of nine, I was raised on an army post outside of Washington, D.C. where every adult male was a soldier, and they were all young. When Dad was transferred to Plattsburg Barracks in upstate New York, a new type of person came into my life—old ones. I hadn't known old people except when we visited a couple called Grandmother and Grandfather. But we only went to see them occasionally.

One day not too long ago, my daughter brought me a bowl of chili, sort of like delivering Meals on Wheels in Mexico. I noticed a name on tape at the top: "Grampa." I wasn't a grampa to her, but I was to her two children. I guess, in her mind, I was the same as one of the old people we used to visit when I was young. That, literally, made me feel like an old man. I got wondering what the word *literally* meant, so I looked it up in my dictionary. The meaning according to Webster had to do with being true. That made me realize I wasn't just a grandfather, but even a great-grandfather. When I was a kid, my great-grandparents were called my ancestors, so I was one now. I looked up the word *ancestor*. According to Webster an ancestor is the progenitor of a group. I did not look up *progenitor*, but now I know what I really am to my great-granddaughter, Payton. Don't laugh; someday you may be a progenitor, too.

In Plattsburg, we lived in town instead of on an army post. Old people walked by our home and, occasionally, I'd see them elsewhere. In our church, my brother, Bob, and I discovered they were slower getting up from the prayer boards than normal people. We'd have made bets on which ones took the longest to get back in their seats, but we had no money except what we were given to put in a basket being passed around. I had no idea I'd ever be just as slow getting up.

As a teen, being young was normal. I was never going to age. The present was all there was—no future, no past. I never envisioned growing up and being six feet tall. No way were corn flakes going to build the arms and legs of an adult on this kid. If my body ever was to achieve a major change, it probably would become a bean. That's what my mother said I'd be someday, "A long string bean." Mom usually told the truth, but I've never seen pods forming on my body.

Later in life, I somehow became a teen (not a bean) at Squantum, Massachusetts. I had no recollection of getting to age thirteen, only of being there, so again I was trapped in the present. I was happy, assuming I'd spend the rest of my life at that age and size. Who wouldn't be happy being thirteen on Squantum, when it was such a remarkable place to live, a one-square-mile island in Boston Harbor? Almost every warm day my brother, Bob, and I spent hours in the water down the hill from our house. We enjoyed swimming there and occasionally had the opportunity to flip away turds, gifts the city of Boston delivered to the bay.

After my dad went to war, my mother, my two brothers, and I moved to Lebanon, Missouri with my new sister, who looked like an Indian. As a teen, I stood almost all the way because the Greyhound bus was full of soldiers going home before heading to war. Then boom—there I was a fifteen year old junior in high school. Once again my world was life in the present tense. It never occurred to me that I'd ever be older. All of my friends acted as if they felt the same.

I ran a mile downtown to see what it was like. Two blocks down a hill, after crossing Highway 66, I passed a dilapidated, old building. Two dilapidated, old people sat out front in dilapidated, old kitchen chairs. Nailed to the wall above the front door was a sign that read OLD FOLKS HOME. The sign made sense. The house was old, the chairs were old, and the two people looked as old as my grandfather and grandmother—perhaps as old as I look to teens today.

Being a worldly-wise fifteen-year-old, I still accepted old people as being less fortunate members of humanity who had been born that way. It never occurred to me that Mom and Dad hadn't always been old, although I'd seen photographs of them as children.

I didn't give much thought to the aging process except to wish I was old enough to join the army. I realized that someday I'd be able to drive a car, but Dad sold ours when he went to war. As a high school junior, I accepted my age, but my brother, Bob, was lucky—two years older, he joined the air corps and got to go to war. Life for me was school, homework, running around with friends, keeping my room reasonably clean, and wishing I was older. Aging was theoretical.

I don't know how it happened, but suddenly my age jumped all the way to forty, and it was just as normal as being a teen had been. Somehow I had become a veteran of the navy, and the army, a college graduate, a husband, and a father. Forty was a pretty good age. I could still do just about anything I'd been able to do in my previous life, and had the advantage of participating in activities I'd never been allowed to enjoy up to then. My wife and I were able to buy our first home, which had a garage to protect our own new car. We had two sons in elementary school, and Jenny, who lay in her little carrier in the middle of the table as we ate. I figured that lifestyle would last forever, though I realized our kids were actually growing older.

One dry, calm day, I was jarred by a bolt of lightning. I'd placed my lunch order at a restaurant and looked around the room to see who I knew. No face was familiar, but one caught my eye. Across the aisle and two tables down, a good-looking blonde in her twenties was glancing around, too. Our eyes met, and I smiled, expecting her to return it, as women usually did. But she gave me the disgusted look young people give when they see old people kissing, then turned her head away. Right then I knew I had traveled the path from Casanova to old fart.

A few years slipped by, and one day, I asked Jenny to come to the office to help prepare calendars to mail to clients. "Sure," she said, "if I can bring my friend, Elsa, along." That night Jenny stuffed, and Elsa put on stamps, while I applied address labels. Everything was cool until Elsa looked at me and said, "Do you have any more stamps, Pops?"

I slept fitfully that night, not realizing I had only witnessed the tip of a giant icicle, which would keep me shivering forever. Being called "Pops" should have been, as they say in the movies, a Preview of Coming Attractions. But I still thought old people only looked old.

If I were ever to get old, I'd just get a few strands of gray. I knew what my wife called crow's feet at the corner of my eyes, were the result of squinting from having fired the rifle in the army. Age wasn't the problem—Elsa was. I wasn't old—she just made me feel like I was.

Though I continued to see minute changes in my life, I still didn't realize old people's bodies slowly crapped out on them, and it was about to happen to me. Soon after Elsa's endearing remark, a problem appeared out of the blue. I'd always been proud of my ability to pee from one edge of a sidewalk to the grass on the other side without getting the concrete wet. That changed. I was no longer able to do the remarkable feat I'd been accustomed to in the simple process of taking a leak. At the age I was then—and I don't know what it was—I figured it wasn't normal.

I didn't know what a urologist did for a living, but it disgusted me to have to make an appointment with one. Fortunately, none of my friends saw me go into his office. It really wasn't good fortune—I made sure none of them were nearby. The guy in the white coat asked a couple of questions then had me give a demonstration sans sidewalk. After I gave it my best effort, he laughed and said, "Your pipes are just getting rusty. It's part of the aging process." He charged me sixty dollars for that professional diagnosis.

Within weeks, Jenny joined in the attack. In my own home, while we were engaged in a supposedly friendly father-daughter conversation, she said something about my bald spot. I excused myself and sneaked to the bathroom to turn my head every which way, looking for a bald spot. I grabbed my wife's hand mirror, held it to my face, and backed up to the image on the door of the medicine cabinet. Getting a glimpse of the back of my head, all I saw was a little area where the hair was pulled away. I went back to the living room to tell her she was nuts, and found she'd left, so I couldn't criticize her for making such an unreasonable mistake.

Then came the deluge, bit by irritating bit. I don't know my exact age when it happened—I had quit counting. The cashier in a grocery store called me, "Sir", and asked if I qualified for a senior citizen discount. I felt like punching her in the nose. Also about that time—or maybe it was only that I'd just began to notice—people started calling me "Mr. Kline" when they knew perfectly well my name was Phil. Once more I accepted my age as normal, expecting to spend the rest of my life in my sixties. Except, I figured sooner or later a booming voice would come from above to proclaim, "Fooled you, didn't I? You thought you were going to be old," and in a puff of smoke, I'd revert to age fifteen. I listened constantly, but the voice never came.

I drove from Michigan to visit Barbara, my younger sister, the one who resembled an Indian when she was born. She and her husband had got to the point where they acted older than I was, and they spent time at the new Old Folks Home, which was now called a Senior Citizen Center.

Old people didn't live there. People who called themselves "seniors", ate, played games, or just sat around and talked there. I visited the center with Barbara and Tom and saw the place had its own bookstore. I went in to determine what was available that told about the aging process, so I could find out what to look forward to that hadn't already attacked me.

I found books with information on high blood pressure, heart, and prostate problems, arthritis, hearing loss, cataracts, and reduced sexual activity. I knew all that—everybody at the center knew all that. I checked the information on the back covers and, as I'd have guessed, the authors were doctors, younger than I was. They all made the same recommendation: "See your doctor".

The one subject, which interested me, was sexual activity. I knew frequency would become a problem, but being single, what was on my mind, was not how often, but when and with whom.

I'd finally accepted the fact that old people weren't born old, and I wanted to locate a book that described all those nasty little changes in life I could look forward to as I aged, changes which wouldn't kill me, but only piss me off. I didn't want to find out why a fart would slip out in front of a Dale Carnegie class. I didn't want to know how face lifts make people seem younger to others. I wanted to learn about those annoying conditions other folks had, which might be waiting around the corner to grab me, the simple ones that doctors didn't write about, such as when the urologist charged me five dollars a word to tell me my problem was part of aging.

I'm not concerned about becoming a resident of an Alzheimers ward, although about a year ago I was close to one. I went to a hospital to get a blood test. I didn't know where the lab was so I asked for directions. From the information I got, I wound my way down a maze of hallways and staircases and found it. After my blood was taken, I headed back through halls and up staircases to get to the parking lot. Somehow I took a wrong turn. I was about to ask directions from a woman sitting at a desk near a set of open double-doors, but before I spoke, I noticed the sign above the doors: ALTZHEIMERS WARD. No way was I going to tell her I was lost. I wished her a happy Monday, retreated down the hall, and eventually found my way out of the building.

The reason I mention that tale is because it seems everyone I know, who is my age, has a story they feel obligated to tell about how they became disoriented, opened the wrong door, or encountered a problem associated with memory loss. If they can't recall a story, they make one up or tell a joke. In the next chapter, I'll mention some of the problems I've had with memory, or I should say, without memory. I promise to keep it short, depending on how much I remember.

Before I continue about me, I want to tell you about my first car, which was built a year before I was. My 1926 Chevrolet and I have had pretty much the same problems as we aged. I bought the car at the age of nineteen when I got out of the navy, so we were close to the same age when we met (I was in the navy during WW II and in the army during The Korean War). Being a car rather than a person, nevertheless it had problems similar to those I've developed since I've grown old (as my granddaughter claims). Listed here are a few of the similarities:

* Young girls are not impressed with the old style body. Guys endure the style, and some of them even want to own a body that looks like mine.

* Rust is an ongoing problem, popping up occasionally. Not only is it impossible to match the original paint, but parts are not easy to come by.

* Hoses are a particular problem. All old parts, which carry liquids, sooner or later, leak.

* Hard to start sometimes, and high gear doesn't work, so a speedometer is of no value.

* Headlights are dimmer than they were originally.

* Steering is a big problem. A big cause of major repairs of an old car or a person is losing control and running into something. Many times repairs cannot be made, so a reasonable alternative is it being sent to the junkyard. I'd hate to do to my body what I did to my car. I put money into repairing a dent then had a wreck the next week, which sent it to the junkyard.

I still wanted to learn how to solve the multitude of problems that would attack me. I went to a library where I found the same books as those at the Senior Citizen Center, written by doctors, on medical conditions related to aging, such as cancer, high blood pressure, arthritis, and all that stuff again. I didn't find one book covering what I wanted to learn. That's when I decided to write a story about the wonderful events I'd suffered, so others would know what they could look forward to. I forgot to write it way back then, but now that I'm in my eighties, this is it.

Before I talk about problems that come with aging, regardless of whether you realize it or not, there are benefits to growing old. For me, most of them come because of women. I happen to like women, but living alone, I miss the close companionship and the multitude of other benefits that go with that sort of thing. One I got was when I went to a book signing of a good-looking blonde I know. I had never hugged her, nor done anything extra-friendly with her other than shake hands. When I walked up to her that night, I got a warm hug, right in front of her husband.

One of the nice things about old age is that I get hugs from young women. Probably because I'm old they don't have to worry about seeming to come on to me. Another benefit, which has astounded me, is that for the first time in my life there are many good looking women around. This last couple of weeks, I have come across at least four good lookers in their late fifties or sixties. One of them, who I believe is happily married, stopped in my classroom at the college after I taught my last session at age eighty-five, to wish me bon voyage and ask me to lunch.

After eating lunch, I picked up the check, and she indicated she had to buy the next time. I'm sure neither of us is interested in a permanent or even a temporary relationship, but it was nice to be able to view a good looking woman as I ate, which I did throughout the meal. After I opened her car door, she hugged me. If I'd been a cat, I would have purred. I may have done so anyway.

Switching from women that cause me to purr, to things that attack the body as we grow old, I must mention that over the years, friends have told me about problems they've had, while others have given me insight into how to solve the scourges of aging without having to pay a doctor to tell them they're old. One of the greatest comments was based on the Alcoholic Anonymous saying of being able to change what we can, having the ability to accept things we cannot change, and the wisdom to know the difference (I'm not an AA member; friend told me that).

Esther Luttrell had previously been a screenwriter for CBS. Recently, when she heard I was writing a booklet about how to get the job you'd love, she sent me an email about the time she was telling a friend how she'd always wanted to work for MGM. When the friend asked if she had ever applied for employment there, Esther said, "No." That motivated Esther to apply for a job at the MGM Studio in Hollywood. She was hired and eventually became a director and producer as well as a screenwriter. In her email Esther wrote, "No matter what your age, you should seek to become what you've always wanted to be. Today you are older than you have ever been, but as young as you will ever be."

I met Esther when she was in her seventies. Five years ago, after hearing her talk about writing at a writers conference in Missouri, I told her she was a great speaker. She said she didn't realize she was that good but had decided to try it out. I knew she was a great speaker and could become a member of The National Association of Speakers. I had started speaking nationally when in my sixties, and she was better than I was. She decided to become a national speaker, and since then, she's spoken in dozens of cities throughout America. She also decided she could write mysteries, and to date has five mystery novels published nationally.

Remember what Esther said: "Today you are older than you have ever been, but as young as you will ever be." Remembering that phrase, may keep me from growing old ungracefully.

TWO

I Believe MEMORY Was Next

Most of the memory problems I have are what I call belated recall. When trying to think of a name or a word, I usually come up with something reasonably close within a few minutes or a few days. One morning my phone rang and woke me at 8:30 (old people sleep late). It was my next door neighbor, John. "What's our mail lady's name?" he asked. I knew her name and never had a problem remembering it before, but John hadn't asked it right. I knew it was the same as that of the wife of the basketball coach at Michigan State University, but because John had asked the question in the wrong manner, I couldn't remember his or her name, so I said, "She has the same name as our basketball coach's wife." John thanked me for my time and hung up.

Minutes later, I remembered that both women were named Lupe, and I remembered the coach's name, Tom Izzo. My not being able to answer John's question wasn't poor memory, but a problem of recall. If he had possessed the common sense to put the question to me in multiple choice—like Mary, Lupe, Ruth, or Kyleigh—I would have been able to recall her name.

Payton is my first great-granddaughter. I know her name but, as I may have stated in Chapter One, every time I want to talk about her, I have to think for a moment to recall her name. The problem of not instantly recalling names extends to my kid's names at times and, once in a great while, to Rosie's, whom I think I've gone with for more than ten years. I don't forget their names, but when talking about them, I should hesitate to make sure I say them correctly.

Just plain words also disappear from my vocabulary, sometimes permanently. One day I was trying to think of the word for the quality in food that helps people achieve regularity. I gave up (recalling the word, not trying to become regular) until I wrote about the recall problem. I must confess I got up, went to the kitchen and read what it said on the side of the bran flakes box: By multiple choice, I chose FIBER. I knew it wasn't FAT, SODIUM or SUGAR. If John had given me four names to choose from, I'd have been able to answer his question. If you have a question about what I write, put it to me in multiple choice and I may be able to answer it, but maybe not.

As long as I'm on the subject of regularity, I may as well discuss that problem. Over breakfast at Mike's Restaurant, Rosie (I know her well enough not to forget her name) (usually) told how some old people announce to their friends that they'd had a bowel movement that morning. I looked at the sowbelly and eggs I was eating and made a decision right there and then to start breaking my overnight fast with high-fiber cereals. Since then, I've alternated between bran flakes, Cheerios, shredded wheat, and another high-fiber cereal I forgot the name of. Why don't those old people Rosie spoke of do that? The message is plastered all over cereal boxes.

Regularity was a fairly easy problem for me to solve by eating high fiber foods. Most problems that have latched onto my body are here to stay. When I was young and had a health problem, either it would cure itself with time, or I'd go to a doctor and have it fixed. Not so, now that I'm old. Most of what has happened to me these past few years hasn't killed me, but I've had to get used to it because it isn't going to go away by itself or with a doctor's help. Wouldn't it be _____ if I end up in the old folk's home in Lebanon, and have young people think I'd been born old? (In case you hadn't noticed, I forgot the word, which means to serve me right).

I was supposed to do a later chapter about memory loss, but as long as I'm here, I may as well keep going. You can skip this part if you've reached the age of sixty or if you've experienced senior moments (the term old people use when they forget something). What I can do is tell some of the memory problems I've had, and if you've already experienced them, or don't have a good reason to read about them, steal a crayon from your grandkid and line out what I write.

Here's a problem I had that you've probably experienced: I went to the front room to get something. Once there, I didn't remember what it was I went to get. I came back to the computer and got to thinking: *I'd better write down the date of Rosie's birthday so I don't forget it.*

That jogged my memory, and I remembered that I had gone to the other room to wrap her present. So back to the front room I went but couldn't locate the present, a locket holding a grain of rice, which had her name written on it, followed by the symbol that stands for heart. I'd bought her the charm at an art show two weeks earlier and put it where she wouldn't stumble across it, but in a place where I could easily locate it. I looked at my calendar and confirmed that her birthday was only three days away, so I had to find it soon. I couldn't get another as the art show was long gone, and I'd forgotten the name of the guy who had made the locket. After checking every hiding place in the front room, I looked in my office and in the bedroom. No luck.

The present was small, so I thought maybe I'd put it in a bowl in the desk drawer where I kept paperclips. I opened that drawer, but the bowl that held them wasn't there. Then I remembered I had only put the bowl in a drawer because, when it was on top of my desk, my Siamese cat had loved to reach in and distribute paperclips around the room. After the cat died of old age, I'd returned the bowl to the top of the desk. I checked and, in it, found the vial that contained a grain of rice with a heart after the name, Rosie. I had put it in plain sight so I wouldn't forget where it was. The moral to the story: If you have to hide something, don't do it. Either that or write yourself a note where you hid it, and remember where you put the note.

Another story that has to do with getting old, may have nothing to do with memory, but just with being of a different generation, although it happened because the guy in the story and I are both old. It wouldn't have been appropriate if we hadn't been old, and if it hadn't been somewhat about memory.

Roger is the leader of The Blue Echoes, a musical group, which got inducted into the National Rock-a-Billy Hall of Fame. We were talking about cars one day and discovered it used to be that when we saw one, we knew the name and the year it was built. Now that we've aged, both of us have to look at the name on the rear of the car to know the make, then guess what year it was made (but the story I want to tell, is about music, not cars).

One of us, I forget which one, was reading a chart of the top twenty songs in the country. I think I was the one because I complained to him that I didn't recognize the names of any of the songs. He said, "Let me see the list." I handed it to him, and after looking it over, he said he'd never heard of any of them either. I was stunned. Roger still plays with The Blue Echoes, and they play a lot of rock. I have a hundred or so seventy-eight r.p.m. records, a couple hundred forty-fives, and at least a hundred of the thirty-three r.p.m.s and I used to know all the songs and the artists who played them. The problem is simply that Roger and I are both old.

I'm sure you've read about and perhaps even experienced memory loss. Years ago I bought the book, *Intelligence and Giftedness*, by Miles D. Storfer. While writing this stirring diatribe, I couldn't remember the name of the book or the author until I pulled it off the shelf. I recall he'd written in the book that people of high intelligence have a problem remembering faces. I recalled that statement because I have a problem remembering faces. I'm more ready to believe it's because I'm intelligent rather than because I'm old.

My memory is still pretty much intact except for the problem I have with names, faces, and titles of songs without words. I usually remember the women I married, but have a difficult time recalling the names of people I met last week. As I stated, facial recall is a problem for me, probably do to my high intelligence, but I have pretty much solved the problem of name remembering by making an association based on their names. By doing so, I usually remember names for a few days—not perfect, but better than before (if I remember to do it).

I had such a great memory in school, I never had to take notes and could still get an "A" on my tests. Numbers always intrigued me, and I could remember them easily. I still remember my navy serial number, my enlisted and officer serial numbers, and my veterans number from when I attended Michigan State University over sixty years ago. I even remember our phone number when I was twelve. Now, I have to write phone numbers down and check them as I dial to get them right. There are times even *that* doesn't keep me from getting wrong numbers.

I have solved the problem of my going into the next room, then wondering why I did so. I've found it helps if I say out loud what I'm looking for. If you come up with a solution that works better, write and tell me the trick, but remember to remind me what problem I wrote about that you solved, if you remember what it was I asked you to help me with. I use the saying it out loud method of remembering every time I remember to use it. When I do say things out loud it works so well that it bugs me when I recall something and wonder why I wanted to remember it.

THREE

THE ITCH
AND OTHER PROBLEMS YOU MAY FACE

One thing that happened years ago (I'll write about it now in case I forget it), I was playing tennis with a pediatrician friend of mine. After playing a set, I sat in the clubhouse scratching my back when he said something dumb like, "Have an itch?"

I told him of a newfound problem of having itchy bumps on my back and on my chest.

He acted as if he was interested in hearing more, so I kept talking. "I didn't remember being stung by insects so I checked my bed to make sure I didn't have bedbugs. I knew they existed because I remembered the nursery rhyme, 'Sleep tight, and don't let the bedbugs bite.' My sheets were not immaculate, but they had no bugs, at least of the bedbug genre."

My friend sounded like the doctor he was when he said, "Those aren't bites—dry skin. It happens when people get old." Then he gave me a glimpse into the golden years. "As you age, little bumps appear on different parts of your body. My patients don't have

23

them; they're too young. A few weeks ago, a dermatologist friend of mine removed more than a hundred of them from a woman about your age. You should see a dermatologist."

I'd never had itchy bumps before except from ticks, chiggers, or mosquitos, so I asked him for the name of a dermatologist, and he recommended a woman whom he said was pretty good. He didn't say at what, but I figured it was for curing itchy bumps. I scratched again and said, "Thanks for the recommendation and for telling me I'm old."

The woman he referred me to may have been "pretty good", but not at problem solving. When I told her about the itches, she asked what doctor had referred me. When I told her his name, she said, "He's a pediatrician." After I informed her that I only play tennis with him, she asked me to take off my shirt. After I did, she inspected my back and chest and confirmed that I was an old man, and that I'd better get used to itching. She also gave me a body lotion and a prescription to relieve the itch. Fortunately, at that time, I was still able to reach all parts of my body, so I was able to apply both. Unfortunately they didn't work that well.

Reach, or the lack of it, is another story I won't go into, except to say I can no longer reach some portions of my body, such as the middle of my back. No problem, except my back is where I have the most itches, evidently not much different from everybody else. Even my grandchildren *uhh* and *ahh* when I scratch their back. Reach is as big a problem for me as the actual itch. My motivation for aspiring to apply my own anti-itch lotion is the same as the reason I go through the donning of my socks in the morning—I have to, similar to having to tie my own shoe laces. Since I've had a stroke, I understand why rich guys used to hire valets to help them dress. Maybe they still do. I wonder if my dermatologist would be "pretty good" at doing that.

On my next visit to my personal doctor, I told him what I'd learned from the dermatologist. "Don't worry," he said. "All your test results show you're in good shape for your age." His comment reminded me of the optometrist I referred my wife to, who told her, "You have pretty good eyes for a woman your age." She never went to him again. I just figured both doctors attended the same medical school as the doctor who charged me five dollars a word to tell me I was old. Obviously none of them ever read *How to Win Friends and Influence People.*

I went to another bookstore to find out what aging problems I could look forward to instead of being surprised by them one at a time. I found nothing about pipes getting rusty, or itchy bumps.

I changed dermatologists, and the new one, who was old, recommended a cream rather than the lotion I'd used on the recommendation of the "pretty good" woman. She also suggested that at my age, I didn't need to shower every day unless I'd performed violent exercise or mowed the lawn. If you're close to me when you read this, you'll believe me when I say I've complied with her recommendation.

Of course, I'm kidding about smelling bad. I don't shower every day, but I do wash under my armpits and my crotch, so people won't be too offended by the stink. The practice of not taking a shower every day has reduced the bumps, but it causes a problem if I don't take one before I go dancing with Rosie, especially during the slow ones when I hold her close. Big deal. Someday when she gets itchy bumps, she'll stink as bad as I do.

By the way, I didn't use another female dermatologist simply to get a buzz from showing parts of my body to a woman. I don't know you, so do it if it turns you on.

There are TV commercials that feature people who have eye problems, but they never address my particular concern. My problem has been that my eyes have excess water in them. I still visit the optometrist who infuriated my wife by telling her that her vision was great for a woman her age. He told me it was normal for eyes to water and that my problem was probably caused by the little drainage ditches next to the eyes being plugged up. I understand these ditches can be cleaned out fairly easily, so I asked him to tell me if he could do it. He said he'd refer me to an ophthalmologist who could tell me if it really was my drains being plugged, or if it was the little folds of skin that had grown next to my eyelids, that caused the problem. If it was the fault of excess skin, maybe I needed a facelift.

The ophthalmologist, who checked me out, put eye drops in my eyes. When he did, I tasted them, so I reasoned that the drains weren't plugged up. Then he gave me a sample of eye drops to use for a couple of weeks. He didn't tell me why I was to add liquid to my eyes when the problem I had was too much liquid in them. I guess I've lost a portion of my intelligence since I got old, either that or doctors who work with vision, are just plain strange.

I complained to the optometrist who sent me to him, and he told me to put drops in my eyes four times a day for a month, then call him and tell him the results. I did what he told me, and it worked to reduce the extra liquid in my eyes almost completely, almost as well as the practice of rinsing my eyes with warm water every morning. I continue using the drops every day and have very little problem with eyes that drip. It showed me that the problem was not that I'm so intelligent, and that those who work with vision know a little bit more about curing an eye problem than I do.

I went to a doctor and showed him a sore on my nose, which he diagnosed as basil cell, a candy-stripe form of skin cancer. He said he'd operate on it but wouldn't remove all the cancer at one sitting. He said I'd have to come back again and again for him to finish the job. If he took all of the cancer off at one time, my nose would be disfigured. I agreed, and he cut the rest of the cancer off over three years without changing my looks, except when I wore a Band-Aid on it.

Actually, my nose was already disfigured from fighting. Some kids near where we lived in Plattsburg, smelled of kerosene, and the biggest one of the pack said his mother put it on his head so he wouldn't get lice. I told my mom what he said, and she told me, "She puts kerosene on his head because he already has lice." I told the kid what my mom had said, and he broke my nose with one punch. Another time it got even more disfigured, was when I played cards on the ship with a hick sailor who was big and mean. I accused him of cheating. I shouldn't have.

The doctor who trimmed the cancer from my nose, talked about how I got the skin cancer. It was because, when outside, I never used sunscreen or wore a baseball cap to guard my nose from the sun. When I go out now, I put on sunscreen or wear a baseball cap. I don't wear it backwards as is the style of today's young people. If you prefer to be in style by wearing your baseball hat backwards, you'll have your nose cut someday. Call me to get my doctor's name. He won't disfigure your face by cutting the cancer all off at once. Better yet, wear your cap the way it was meant to be worn.

Growing Old Ungracefully / Phil Kline

FOUR

OTHER THAN MEMORY
BUT INCLUDING MORE MEMORY

My fingernails get cracks in them and snag the sweaters, socks, or garments old people wear. I trim them, but soon they grow back with more cracks. In addition to fingernails developing cracks that snag, my toenails tend to curl up—they not only tend to do so, they actually do it. I can usually cut them back without drawing blood, but they are difficult to reach. I expect I'll have to visit a pedicurist sooner or later—probably sooner. I don't know what I'll do about the blood tattoos that cover my ankle, the varicose veins on my legs that embarrass me, or the arthritis in my toe.

I get up two or three times a night to take a pee. I live alone, so nobody knows about that except you, so don't tell anyone. When I stand after having been in bed, I have to hold onto the wall to make sure I don't join the other old people at the emergency room of our local hospital who are there for the same reason. Even my new dermatologist was using a cane the last time I saw her. When I asked why, she said she fell and broke her hip. If I were to fall and break my hip at this age, it would take three times as long for it to

29

heal than it did when I was young. Also, when I fell as a young man, I didn't break anything. It just hurt for a day or two. Actually, the two times I broke my arm after experiencing a fall on my bike, I kept riding with my arm in a sling.

People say, "Thank you for your service," when I tell them I lost my hearing from serving in the artillery. Hearing loss comes in handy when people talk about things I don't want to hear, and even more so when I still had my Siamese cat. It was nice not having to listen to his yowling.

I sleep until nine most every morning, but don't get up right then. I'll explain why in a future chapter. Right now, I'll go back to writing about memory loss before I forget to. Actually it's not a complete loss. I remember the names of the people I went to high school with seventy years ago, and not only the names of the popular songs of that era, but the words to them, including such favorites as, *When Yuba Plays the Rhumba On The Tuba Down in Cuba, Two Fat Polka,* and *It Takes A Long Tall Brown-skinned Gal To Make A Preacher Lay His Bible Down.* I remember the words to most of the old songs, but even forget the names of songs that don't have words. I understand that is normal as we age. I read that there are two little short-term memory portions of the brain that go first, and cause "senior moments."

A few days ago, I was trying to learn the words to *You Are My Flower* by Lester Flatt and Earl Scruggs (I looked up their names). I wanted to learn the words so I could sing them to my ex-wife who was in town visiting our daughter. She hated the words of the song and even the names Lester Flatt and Earl Scruggs. After a half hour of working on the words, I got to the point I knew them, but couldn't keep them going while singing so I didn't sing to her. That story proves beyond a doubt that my problem is not loss of memory, but only that of putting new information into an old brain, which is rusting away like my 1926 Chevy.

Don't ask me to give you directions or to dial phone numbers. I mess them up. I understand there's a section of the brain solely designed to make it difficult for old people to remember names and numbers, so it isn't my fault. Also when reading a story, I have to concentrate on remembering the different characters. I can tell you what day of the week it is only by looking at a white board, which hangs to the left of my desk. It records what I have going on for three weeks. People are amazed that I can tell them what today's date is and what I have going on for the next twenty-one days. But don't ask me to recall my passwords.

Let me tell you about writing down phone numbers or poking them while making calls (I use the word "poking" because nobody's ever come up with an acceptable word to describe how to get a number by pushing buttons). I get my numbers mixed up. Every once in a while, when I call Rosie, John answers. He's not at her house—I dialed the wrong number. Numbers are bad. It was April or May before I started writing 2014 on my checks. In fact, it took until this year to quit starting the year with nineteen. You can expect to have the same problem someday.

A problem related to memory loss, which has crept up on me, had to do with my getting hung up on the computer (not physically but mentally). Computers were a piece of cake when I was young and they could only perform simple functions, but now they're complicated. The makers of computers caused problems by manufacturing products to perform more unnecessary functions than their competitor's. The newer machines have become more complicated, so the builders have to inundate us with complicated directions. That's not the only problem—I switched to an Apple, which meant I had to buy *The Little Mac Book* to learn the new way to do stuff after I had already partially mastered doing it the older, simpler way. The book was too complicated for me to understand. That brings up another problem that will come along to mess up your mind as old age grabs you—the inability to understand directions.

Anyone who lives long enough will experience that amazing development along with a newfound loss of memory. Put in language old farts can understand: I expect you will develop a problem comprehending normal directions, some of which you now consider as being so simple, even a child can understand them.

I sometimes solve the newfound problem of not understanding simple directions by writing them down on a 3 x 5 card and speaking them out loud, but the best solution I've come up with is to put Rosie in charge of directions.

I still know how to drive a car as long as it doesn't have all the new concepts I don't understand. I even have a problem in that my car tends to remember where it went last time and wants to follow the same familiar path, rather than the one I want. A couple of days ago, I was headed to the car fix-it place, and my car was about to take a turn that would take me to a restaurant in the opposite direction, the one where I was going the following day to have lunch with a good-looking blonde. Perhaps it was poor direction finding on my part, or maybe my Jaguar would rather have had a blonde sit on its lap instead of knowing a mechanic would be tinkering with it. But then, maybe the Jag was anticipating having the blonde tinker with it.

Another bit of great advice you may get from this chapter is this: "If you have a problem understanding something about your computer, ask a child to help you." Of course you realize you have to be quick about getting help from younger people. Don't wait too long. Someday they'll get old, and when they do, they'll have the same trouble as you.

I have yet to completely solve the problem of going to the next room, then wondering why I did so. It helps if, on the way, I say out loud my reason for going there (did I write this before?) Anyway, if you come up with a better solution for that minor problem, write and tell me the trick, but again remind me what problem you solved that I asked you to help me with. There is a benefit to that minor lapse of memory; the exercise I get from walking back and forth between rooms while trying to remember why I was making the trip in the first place.

Losing memory has been a real problem for me. In high school and college, I was an actor of sorts. With the great memory I had then, I knew everybody else's lines and helped them when they faltered. A few years ago, when I acted in a play for a community theatre, it took forever to remember my own lines. I don't have to learn the words anymore—I quit acting.

Installing new stuff in my brain is one of my greatest memory problems. I'm sure that someday you'll have the same problem of memory installation when you find the inbox box to your memory is locked. You'll discover for yourself that people grow old in everything, not just in looks.

This book is not all about problems; there are solutions, such as my friend has. He can't remember if he brushed his teeth so he touches his toothbrush to see if it's wet. I have another friend who says he forgets to zip up his fly before leaving the bathroom. The good side of what he said was, "I immediately know when I've forgot to unzip before taking a leak."

To solve one type of memory loss, if you remember to do so, recall my method: When I go to the next room to get something and want to remember what I went to get, or if I'm opening a cupboard door and don't want to wonder why, I speak out loud the name of whatever it is I was looking for. In grammar school, my teacher said we remember better if we vocalize it, like remembering someone's name by using it. Next time you go to the window to check the outside temperature, say, "Temperature." On the way to the cupboard to get a cup, say, "Cup".

The problem is remembering to say the word that tells why I'm going there. Recalling names is more difficult. If I ignore the loss, usually within a short period of time the name will pop into my head—if not, I look it up. When I do determine the correct name, I relate it to a rhyme or story. For instance: If I need to remember the name of a man named Kelly, I picture a fat Irish desk-cop. All desk-cops are overweight and they're all named Kelly. Jenny Drumkowski was simple. I pictured my daughter, Jenny, going down a hill on skis with a cow that played drums.

When I decided to write about the song, *It Takes A Long Tall Brown-skinned Gal To Make A Preacher Lay His Bible Down*, I'd forgot the name of the man who recorded it. I looked on his album—Louis Prima. His real name was probably Luigi, and Prime means number one. He was probably the first Italian to realize that it takes a long, tall, brown-skinned gal to make a preacher lay his bible down—Louis Prima. One of my neighbors made remembering easier. Jessie married a woman named Jessie. Now neither of us will ever forget her name.

Occasionally, when talking about Jenny, I'll say Ashley, her daughter's name. I haven't forgotten Jenny's name. It's just a sort of malady that infects old people in conversations. I don't like having that particular problem, because often people try to help me overcome it. Forgetting the names of close associates is embarrassing. Don't tell Rosie, but while she was in Texas visiting her grandchildren, I had lunch with a good-looking woman I've known for years. I was in the process of telling her a story about Rosie, but when I got to the point of saying her name, I stuttered, and the woman realized I had forgot Rosie's name. I made a simpleton excuse for my memory lapse and continued with my story, as she snickered.

The absolute best way I know to solve the problem of memory loss is to write things down. If you still forget important things, use pennies to solve the problem of concern you may have. For example: I made the decision that I could reduce the concern over problems that bother me. As a kid, I learned that pennies bring good luck, so on my desk in front of me, I put a penny, then another one on each of the two dressers in my bedroom, one on the desk in the kitchen, and another on the end table next to the easy chair where I read. They are still there years later and remind me how lucky I am to have so few problems. It works for me—maybe it will for you.

One day I found a penny on the sidewalk at the college campus. I picked it up, after recalling the poem I learned in elementary school, "Find a penny, pick it up, and all the day you'll have good luck." Later I saw another and grabbed it, too. My belief that college students won't bend over to pick up a penny was borne out over the next few weeks when I'd see them smile at me as I did so. I may be old, but I'm almost as normal as I used to be.

That story about putting pennies in different locations in my home has much to do with solving a multitude of problems other than memory loss, but rather than bore you with those kinds of details, I'll move on to a more intellectually stimulating subject— such as pain.

FIVE

PAIN

Many Tuesday nights, Rosie and I go dancing at the local VFW hall. That placates her as much as anything I can still do. Tom, the leader of a group of five musicians who played there, was older than the others. He played guitar and sang most of the vocals. Then, one night Tom was replaced by a guy who didn't have the mellow voice I was used to hearing. I wondered why the change. The next time we went dancing, he was still missing. I told a band member I missed Tom, and he said, "He fell and broke his collarbone and an arm."

I should have known. For years I'd read about old guys or old gals falling and breaking a hip or clavicle or whatever. I thought the problem was brittle bones, but the cause is age. I discovered that one morning when I was putting on my pants.

Having been a person slow to realize there's more to growing old than looks, I refused to believe I couldn't stand on one leg for any length of time, so I kept dressing the same way. I kept putting my trousers on without the fear of falling and breaking whatever they call that bone (I'm sure it's not called an ass bone). After falling once, I decided to do that phase of dressing while holding on to the dresser that has the phone on it. I don't make calls while putting on my pants except on rare occasions. The phone just happens to be on the dresser next to where I lay my pants while I sleep. I don't wear them to bed (phone, dresser, or pants). Having the phone nearby is a good idea, in case I fall and need to make an emergency call for help.

Donning a shirt is another story. I don't worry about falling while doing it, but sometimes it causes pain anyway.

The worst situation of all takes place as it did one night when Rosie and I were leaving a dance at the VFW. Some sweet young thing saw I was having trouble putting on my jacket, and she offered to help me. Half of the people there, and all of my friends, saw it happen. That was almost as embarrassing to me as them thinking I would fall while getting dressed. Doing so is possible, since the major cause that sends people to a hospital emergency room, in their golden years, is injuries from a fall. As the years zip by, it becomes important for me to be careful not to do anything to increase the income of an emergency room doctor.

A time when I really have the possibility of falling happens at a dance is when I've been sitting for a while and stand up to head to the dance floor. I know what will happen and am ready to stagger a bit. But one night, when I'd been reading for over an hour, I stood up and fell down. Fortunately, I fell on the sofa. I got to my feet, not realizing I was still unsteady, and my one leg gave way. Unfortunately, this time I fell away from the sofa, to the fireplace, where I banged my shin and my elbow on the bricks. I was lucky not to have broken either. Now I know better than to stand with confidence after sitting for an extended period.

I used to run up and down stairs, but no more. My older brother and his wife are not as smart as I am. Both of them broke bones from falling down stairs, she once, and he twice. I learned from hearing of their misfortune, so I use a bannister every time I go up or down stairs and I do it while creeping like an old man should.

It's also a good idea to put a handrail in your bath and to use it. I wasn't smart enough to know that—Rosie told me to do it. And keep your eyes open as much as possible in the shower. Much of our balance comes from seeing our surroundings, and we lose that advantage when our eyes are closed. Often I reach to a shower handrail to maintain my balance.

Falling is a major reason the bathroom is known as the most dangerous room in the house. A handrail in the shower helps make it a safe place. An astronaut, who went into space successfully, was disabled when he fell while taking a shower. So be careful when you take one, but don't worry if you're not handsome when naked. An advantage to old age is that you don't have to worry about anyone seeing you naked—normal men don't usually sneak a peek at old women in the shower even if the view is worth the effort. I don't know if women do it.

Many older people have pains, which rule their lives, and for one reason or another, most of my friends are old. Many of them have a pain, which curtails their activities. I know because two friends wrote me letters saying they had fallen, which limits what they can do.

I was having lunch with another friend on a Monday when a guy walking by said, "Hello, Phil," and handed me his business card. He had recognized me as having done work for a company he managed years ago in another Michigan city. A day later, I called him to have lunch with me, and we set an appointment for that Friday. He called me Friday morning and said he couldn't make lunch because of a pain in his back he'd gotten from a fall months earlier. We reset lunch a few days later. He looked fine, but walked kind of funny.

Two times in one day, I fell while walking in a light snow, which had a layer of ice beneath it. Fortunately, each time my fall was into deep snow, and I wasn't hurt. I should have learned after the first time it happened. Beware of walking in snow, especially if it has ice under it.

Many times we cause our own falls. A thousand years ago I remember my mother saying, "Quit dragging your feet." I didn't take her advice—I figured it was part of my personality. In today's world, I could blame it on my DNA. Looking back on it, I sort of enjoyed the echo I made by dragging my feet as I walked the hallways at school. For a couple of years in high school, I even wore little steel plates on my heels and toes. But don't you do it. You'll make a cool sound but you'll also make bruises—you pay for the rhythm you create.

When I joined the army in 1948, a drill sergeant convinced me that dragging my feet was not an integral part of marching, so I tried to get rid of the habit, without complete success. Years later, I had carpeting in my home, which at times made me trip when I dragged my feet. But that wasn't as exciting as what happened while walking down the steps from my kitchen to the garage. I'd forgotten about the doorsill the builder put there to make leaving the house an exciting maneuver. I was propelled forward but fortunately I grabbed the doorframe, which kept me from butting a dent in the hood of my twelve-year-old Jaguar—my car—not the jungle cat.

We old people tend to shuffle or drag our feet because it requires less effort than raising them while walking (walking's hard work). I finally became aware of that, and that's when I really decided not to drag my feet. Since concentrating on raising them while walking, other than in the snow, I've only fallen twice this year. Mom would be proud of me.

I used to ride a bicycle up to 100 miles a day, until I was in my seventies. I learned to take it easy on my legs by spinning them when riding long distances. It's smart to use toe-straps. Without them, pedal power comes only from pressing down. With them, power comes from lifting the foot as well as pushing down. While walking, I lift my feet, similar to spinning them while riding a bike—that helps eliminate falls caused by foot-dragging. That's why walking's one thing I'm beginning to do gracefully except when I stroll in the snow.

Falling isn't the only dangerous thing old people do. I told a seventy year old woman that I bit my tongue. She said she does so about once a week. I used to do it as often, but I'm not that bad anymore. I only bite my tongue or cheek about every two or three weeks now. About a year ago, I bit it so hard I had to pay a social call on my surgeon friend to have him sew up the resulting tear. I work on chewing slowly so as to bite the food, not myself. The hiatal hernia I have, helped solve my tongue-biting problem—it made me slow down my chewing so I wouldn't gag.

Strange things happen that surprise me. As I walk down the hall of my house, every once in a while I drift toward a wall, and occasionally I bang the back of one of my hands, leaving a dark purple bruise. I just get one to disappear when I do it again. I banged the back of my left hand on the outside mirror of my Jag. It took the skin off a circle the size of a dime. I covered it loosely to give it air, and saw my doctor to see if I'd handled it properly. He said yes then, with a poor choice of words, explained, "Due to your age, it will take about two weeks to heal." He was close. It took three. When I was a teen, it would have taken three days, or perhaps up to a week when I was in my twenties.

Banging my hand doesn't hurt that much—it just looks bad. Other problems pop up occasionally. Sometimes my morning walk is interrupted by a sudden glitch in one of my feet, knees, or my hip, other than that caused by my stroke. I limp due to this glitch, but keep walking until it goes away—it usually does. I live alone, so nobody sees me hobble from getting old. Sometimes I get dizzy. When I do, I wait it out, and eventually it goes away, too. I mentioned before about what happens when I stand after I've been sitting for a while, being unstable. I told Rosie about that happening, and she surprised me by saying she had the same problem.

Do you know what a rotor-cup is? If not, you may find out someday when you have a problem getting your arm in a shirt or jacket. My doctor recommended a rotor-cup operation. I told other old people what he said, and many of them confessed they'd had it done, and that it was painful. I had mine operated on, but it only hurt during recuperation when I exercised my arm. It doesn't bother me anymore unless I lie on that side while sleeping. Even if you don't have a rotor-cup problem, but have trouble putting on a shirt or jacket, like I said, you'll be embarrassed when young girls offer to help you. It's even worse when old ones do.

Most of the problems I've developed as I age, don't bother me that much. I know the alternative to aging is dying, and I ain't ready to go that route. Certain things, which have happened, make me think, being so old, whether I should have those problems fixed. I feel it would be a waste of money to get some errant body function repaired and die soon after—similar to the time I put a dent in my car a month after I'd canceled my collision insurance.

For a long time I didn't have many pains other than one in my hip that doesn't seem to go away. My hiatal hernia isn't much of a problem. I just have to eat slower than I'm used to, and at other times I have to quit eating and wait for the food to go down my throat. My doctor said, "It's not worth going through surgery at your age." I've often wondered if it was a part of the training curriculum in medical school to tell people they're old.

A problem I do have is with my teeth. When I was a kid, my parents had false teeth and never checked to see if I had brushed mine. So I didn't brush them regularly until I got in the army, when I did so because the other guys did. My childhood neglect made for problems as I grew older. I take good care of them now, but I started doing so too late in life. I had a couple of teeth filled last year to get rid of a bit of rot that took only minutes to drill out and put in amalgam. I asked my dentist why I had cavities when I now take good care of my teeth.

In telling me something I should have known, he started with three words I've heard a few times. "*When you age*, the spaces between your teeth and gums grow larger, causing bits of food to lodge there and cause cavities. Not only should you floss before brushing your teeth, but use a gum brush too." He gave me one, a little wire with small fibers to poke between my gums and teeth to get the last remaining bits of food out. I use it after meals, at night, and during the day if I've had a snack. The next time I went to my dentist, I found that it had worked.

One of the problems I have is poor circulation in my hands and feet. I'm constantly reminded of this when they feel cold or when I shake somebody's hand. Often the person on the other end of my hand will remark how cold it is; it's a lack of proper circulation. Many times my hands get cold and I have to wear gloves when others don't. I've heard that the way to maintain circulation in my hands and my feet is to wear clothes that keep my chest and valuable organs toasty. That way, my blood will realize it can flow to my extremities to keep them warm. At last, women will no longer grab my hand and say those four words, "Your hand is cold."

I've had prostate cancer, but I don't know how you can prevent that. I had mine removed by surgery. The only suggestion I have is to check your options with the surgeon ahead of time. The surgery took away my sexual pleasures in my sixties. The problem was not having surgery - it was the surgeon who didn't use a new technique, which could have let me keep my sex drive in force. Evidently he didn't think sex was that important, at least not for me.

I wear hearing aids and hate them. I can tell you how to prevent the kind of hearing loss I have: *Don't join the army and wear ear plugs when mowing, shooting, or when around other loud noises.*

I can hear people talk but can't understand what they are saying. Women, especially those with high-frequency voices, can talk to me all day without my understanding a word unless they face me (high frequencies travel in straight lines). I nod and smile often and say, "Huh?" a lot. If they're good-looking blondes I may not hear them any better, but who cares so long as they stand close to me to make sure I hear them. Two advantages you may gain with hearing loss are (1) when people bore you with what they're saying, and (2) if you happen to have a Siamese Cat.

Another problem I have, which I can't tell you how to avert, and one you can look forward to, is arthritis. I have it in my neck, wrists, and one toe. Arthritis is something you will probably get as you grow older. I saw a doctor for mine, and he gave me a prescription for the pain. I never used it because of my high pain tolerance. If you use one, only use the amount necessary.

Fortunately, one of the things I thought would happen to me, didn't happen: reduced vision. I don't wear glasses except to make small print easier for me to read.

The doctor, who cut on my nose six times to get all of the cancer off, suggested I use sunscreen when riding the bicycle. For years I had ridden with no shield of any kind for my poor nose. Now when I go out in the sun for any length of time, I make sure I have sunscreen on most of the exposed areas of my body (this may sound familiar, but it's worth repeating)

This is worth repeating, too: Some young people consider wearing their baseball cap backwards to be stylish. It started with gang members who got it from their friends in prison, whose belts were taken away to stop them from beating other prisoners. Baseball caps were designed with a bill to protect players' noses from the sun. The backwards baseball cap invites cancer of the nose. Be prepared to have your nose cut on (or off) if you dress to honor gang members.

The water in my eyes still won't drain well, my nose drips at least twenty or thirty times every day, my fingernails crack, my toenails have curled up and are difficult to reach, blood tattoos

45

cover my ankle, varicose veins are hidden by my socks after I finally get them on (the socks, not the veins). My arthritis doesn't embarrass me—people can't see it. I have to get up two or three times a night to pee, but that doesn't embarrass me—it isn't public unless I forget to close the blinds before crawling into bed. Perhaps it will become public if I fall and my friends read about it in the paper, if they are of the few who still read a newspaper.

Getting up for anything in the middle of the night is scary. Old farts have morning blahs, so their sense of balance is impaired. Perhaps that would a good reason to tell people why I don't get up before nine, unless by mistake I have agreed to meet somebody early in the morning.

There is one thing I wish I could get rid of, but as of right now, I don't know enough about eliminating the problem to give you advice. At a meeting put on by a member of the Michigan Legislature, a man nearby had a drop of water hanging on the tip of his nose. My thought at the time was why he didn't blow his nose. It was only a couple of months later that I discovered the reason it happened to the guy in the meeting, when my own nose began to drip. Now it drips as do the noses of millions of old people around the world. I was telling a woman twenty years my junior about it, when she surprised me by saying she had the same problem as she reached for a handkerchief to wipe a drop off her pretty little nose.

When I eat, my nose drips; when I brush my teeth, my nose drips; when I walk fast; when I mow the lawn or do other work outside, my nose drips; many normal things I do every day cause my nose to drip. It flows like a faucet when I cough, and when I sneeze, more like a river, or at least a good-sized stream. I keep a handkerchief close to the toilet. Nose dripping is one of the things

I've been told to accept, as it's here to stay. A problem is that I tend to act like other old farts and not pay attention when it happens. Someday when you least expect it, you may see some old guy with a drop hanging from the end of his nose. I don't want that guy to be me, but it would be better than having it dripping on his shirt or suit coat.

The worst cause I have for a dripping nose is after I take a drink, or for some other reason, liquid in my mouth goes down the wrong hole and makes me cough. That causes me to sneeze and lose control while trying to dislodge the liquid from my air duct. On top of the gyrations I go through, my eyes water, my nose drips like the stream I mentioned, and I lose control of my upper body. It's bad enough when I'm alone, but causes people close by to wonder if I'm going to make it through the day. Probably the only thing, which could make it worse, is if I lost control of my bowels. That's never happened, and I wouldn't write about if it did.

If you come up with a solution to nose-drip, call me, email me, or in some other way, let me know how you do it, but don't tell Rosie. She complains when it happens to me, so I can hardly contain myself waiting for her nose to start dripping. I think it has, but she hides it. An advantage of having a leaking nose is that I have enough used Kleenex to start the fire in my fireplace.

While editing this diatribe, suddenly I started seeing double, not the side-by-side type but where one eye was seeing the print about three inches above the other. I had to quit editing, but that gave me time to figure out if it was caused by the stroke I had last year or if it was another problem of growing old ungracefully. It was probably a combination of both.

I'll cover other problems, which may be lurking around the corner, or possibly before you even get to the corner. I'm about to give you answers to some bad things that may attack you sooner or later. If I were to include it as a chapter, it would be titled "MOVEMENTS".

SIX

(What the Hell) MOVEMENTS

Once when I was probably younger than you are now, I was talking dumb to a guy half my age that ran marathons. Being a sprinter, not a distance-runner, I bragged that I could beat him running from one end of a parking lot to the other. He laughed and said, "You're crazy." True, but I'd been running races all my life but seldom beat. I knew I could outrun him.

Marathon Man was right—I was off my rocker. We headed to the parking lot and started running, but the race only lasted seconds. My mind ran faster than my legs, and I went down on the asphalt. My body had forgotten what my mind remembered. My mind knew that only a few years earlier, I'd won a race against my roommate, a pitcher for the Michigan State University baseball team. One night while checking out our home brew, he tossed around a few superlatives while telling me he could outrun everyone else on the team. I told him, "You can't outrun me."

He laughed. "I have a dollar bill that says I can beat you down Jerome and back."

We started down Jerome Street at midnight. Soon I was ahead of him and didn't look back. A mile or so later, I glanced back and didn't see him; he had given up, so I just coasted back to the apartment where he gave me a worn-out old dollar bill. The memory of that victory is what caused me to fall on my ass in the parking lot while racing Marathon Man.

It wasn't a year after the debacle of Marathon Man, three young friends and I were playing football on the street in front of my home. My partner threw a pass, and I caught it. I ran with it, but before I reached the edge of the street, my legs decided they couldn't keep up with what my mind told them they could do. I fell and slid on the pavement until my face stopped three inches from the curb. In my mind I still see that rock solid curb about to bust my face.

My mind plays the same type of memory tricks on me when I take Rosie dancing at the Old Folks Home in Eaton Rapids once a month. Before I get to the exciting part, I'll tell you that the people we've met there are a bunch of old farts, so I know that old age snuck up on them. On my mother's eighty-seventh birthday, she told me that the last time she looked, she was seventeen. I don't have to tell you that old farts know old age is instantaneous.

When I was young, I never missed a dance, fast or slow. I did polkas one after the other, with jitterbugs mixed in, and never missed a beat. Now in Eaton Rapids when the band plays a polka, I wait until it's half over before leading Rosie to the dance floor. She kids me about delaying our dance, but she's even worse. I tell people why I wait halfway through the tune, but I've never heard her admit she's glad I do so. If I accused her of agreeing with me in wanting to do half polkas, she'd probably deny it. A night of dancing lasted four hours when I was young. I don't know how long it lasts now. The band is still playing when we leave.

I can do all the dances I used to do as long as I do half-polkas, yet when I walk, I notice it's at a slower pace than it used to be. At the college where I used to teach, I occasionally decided to walk alongside young people on the way to class. At least, I thought I would, until I realized most of them walked faster than I did. But I can dance half-polkas better than they can.

Occasionally I still stumble while walking, even without the steel plates on my toes and heels that made the cool sound. Dragging my feet makes me have to concentrate on lifting them so I don't stumble. But dragging them is still easier than lifting them. Another old fart habit of mine is that I tend to let my mouth hang open (I don't just tend to—I do it) because it takes less energy to let it hang than to keep it closed. I tell Rosie I do so to keep from grinding my teeth.

Driving to and from the Old Farts dance in Eaton Rapids, is a cinch. Once a month I pick her up on the way to the dance. The only problem I have in driving to or from the dance is if I go a different route than usual. As I wrote in a previous chapter, my Jag occasionally likes to take the road where it anticipates a happy experience or when it wants to travel the route it took last time. I have to make sure the car knows I'm in command because we take the correct route only as long as it does what I tell it to do. I have to tell the dumb thing I'm in charge.

A friend from down the street was pulled over by the police one night for doing something wrong (I forget what). He said he told the cop, "What do you expect? I'm eighty-four years old."

I joke about driving, but at eighty-seven, I have no problems as long as I pay attention to what I'm doing. I don't talk on the phone, or even to the person sitting next to me, when I'm in traffic or in a situation where I may have to make a decision. If I keep driving cautiously, I expect I can drive a few more years, but when my driving begins to resemble my running, my dancing, or my lovemaking, I'll quit (P.S. I already quit the lovemaking, courtesy of an idiot surgeon). Don't mention that to anyone else; in fact, forget I said it.

The biggest problem I have at this age isn't as much about walking or running as it is being a Lazy-Good-For-Nothin'. I don't want to do much anymore, including fun things I used to yearn to do. I don't care to spend my life in bed, yet in the morning, I have to convince myself to get up. Then I wonder what I'm going to do all day. It's nice if I need to go to the store, mow the lawn, shovel snow, or do the laundry. That way I don't have to figure out how to plan my day.

I spend a bunch of time in my Lazy-Boy chair. It's nice when one of the magazines, to which I subscribe, arrives. I read instead of sitting and thinking what to do, other than vegetate. The trouble is that when I get out of the chair, it's not painful, just difficult and dangerous. My neighbor, John, has the same problem. He's the guy who says, "Before I bend to pick up something, it's better to wait till I have a couple of reasons to bend that far." He's younger than I am, but his problem is that he never had to pick up stuff during his employment with the State.

I believe most of the problems I have, being a Lazy-Good-For-Nothin', is that there aren't that many things I used to enjoy that I still like to do. I do a few of them simply because I know I should. I used to like to run and ride my bike, but now both of those former pleasures are hard work. The same with dancing, which I used to love—I still like to dance, only not as much. After about an hour, I'm ready to come home and go to bed. Even though it was a regular chore, I used d to enjoy teaching, especially the interaction with adult students. At the age I am now, even writing is something I tend to put off. Perhaps that's why I have lunch with good-looking blondes; it gives me something to do that ain't work, and that I still enjoy, even when Rosie doesn't think I should.

Not enjoying bike riding bugs me more than the loss of any other form of exercise. I used to ride at least four days every week, sometimes more than a hundred miles a day. When I broke my left arm, at around age fifty, I had the doctor fix the sling so I could still ride. I raised my handlebars and lowered the seat in order to make it easier to get on and had to walk five minutes every ten or so miles to ease the pain in my butt. Seven days after I broke the arm, I rode seventy-five miles. After my arm healed, I rode many one-day trips of sixty to a hundred miles for pure pleasure. Over the next three years I rode more than six thousand miles, but as I grew older, riding became less fun until one year I rode only eight hundred miles. The next year the fun was gone, and I rode only eight miles. I've ridden some since then, but the enjoyment's not there anymore. I must be getting old.

My ex-wife and I always wanted to walk the Appalachian Trail, so she and I took a six-day trip, hiking from Springer Mountain in Georgia to South Carolina, a total of over seventy miles. In preparation for that walk, we hiked trails and mountain paths for hundreds of miles, all of it fun. That fun I had hiking with her has departed now that she's gone and even more so because of my age.

Old age has taken away the enjoyment of biking and backpacking. The same lack of fun has ended the highs I used to get from many forms of movement. But I don't yearn for the old days—they gave me many of the memories I treasure.

Perhaps the next segment comes under the title of MOVEMENTS. At least it's related. Perhaps it would be better to have a chapter solely about problems of the mouth, but it would be a short chapter. All I can do is tell you what happened to me, not how to solve the problems. I doubt if anyone who reads this will have the solution to problems where I said the wrong thing, so I won't give you any of them.

A couple of things do happen because of my age. My tongue used to be able to travel around the interior of my upper and lower lips to clear out food. Now it has grown old along with the rest of me and doesn't extend as far as it used to. And I tend to sneeze more.

Many times my sneezing is related to another problem such as after I gag a bit from a liquid going down the wrong hole, or after coughing, which I do more often as I grow older, sometimes as much as five times in one day. If I end up with a good sneezing fit, my nose will drip. I repeat this problem here, not knowing how to explain it gracefully to younger onlookers. If anything, I probably should tell them I inherited it from my mother's DNA or that there's a hidden purpose to it.

One problem has appeared within the last few years, which is related to a mouth, but not to mine. A friend had a disease, which caused her sometimes to dribble her food or drink. She tells about meeting with a young man one time, and while consuming an ice cream soda, she realized he was staring at the portion of it that was traveling down her chin. I write this because someday you may look forward to keeping a napkin handy when eating or drinking. Due to the stroke I had, many times, while drinking, or when I have a fluid in my mouth, a portion will dribble down my chin, so I make sure I always have a napkin handy to hide it from others. Occasionally, not only liquid, but solid food I have in my mouth will slide down the wrong hole. I've experienced this at times throughout my life, but now it occurs more often, causing me to cough uproariously, and make other people wonder if I'm going to last through the day. Usually I manage to tell them between gags, "It went down the wrong hole," if I can get it said before going into a sneezing fit.

Another movement you've seen in old people, if you are still able to see stuff up close, is shaking hands. Not where they compulsively shake hands with you, but where their hands shake when they attempt to grab something or do a task, which requires slow movement of the arm. For instance, this morning as I was attempting to clean leftover food lodged between my teeth, my hand began to shake just enough so that it caused a problem for me to get the brush between my teeth. It kept jabbing the tooth or my gum. Strange, I had not noticed this happening before, but as soon as it occurred, I remembered seeing the same shaking in the hands of old farts a long time ago when I used to be young. I knew what the problem was back then but figured it would never happen to me. Now that it has, I'm mortified that I don't know how to solve the problem.

Something else, not quite as embarrassing, probably will happen to you someday when a person close to you will say, "You have something on your chin." The first time it happens, you may not believe it, but before long, when it becomes a regular happening, you'll know it, and you'll realize you've finally arrived as an old fart. When there's nobody around to say food is hanging on your chin, eventually it will drop. Rosie says she can tell what I had for lunch by the stains I have on my shirt. I should learn to change shirts before dancing with her. Just a week or two ago (I don't remember which), I met an old woman who had a stroke twelve years ago. She told some of the ways it changed her life, most of them I already knew, as they had happened to me. One of the things she shared with me was that her husband had to tell her, during almost every meal, "You have a bit of food hanging from your lip."

Fortunately, or perhaps because I work at my rehab, I maintain most of the jobs I used to do as a volunteer before I had my stroke. I still have a relationship with the ROTC at Michigan State University due to my serving on the Armed Forces Board of The MSU Alumni Association. In preparation to attend the Army Military Ball, I had to wear a suit and tie. After ten minutes of trying to tie a Windsor knot in my tie, I gave up and called my neighbor, John. He couldn't tie a Windsor knot but managed to tie a regular knot for me, so I'd look pretty for the cadets and so Rosie wouldn't crab at me. I looked pretty, but she still criticized.

There's Enough Pain in Aging for Another Chapter

SEVEN

PAIN AGAIN

It pains me not to be able to whistle a tune like I used to, and I can't whistle through my teeth the way I used to whistle at pretty girls. But that's not the type of pain I'm talking about.

Growing old is painful—it hurts—not the actual process of getting older, but some of the things that happen. I have a bunch of friends, not really a bunch, but a few of the guys from my Officers Candidate School are still around. We used to total ninety-six, but only sixteen of us are left. Of course many of those who are no longer around didn't die of old age. Some were killed in action during the Korean War or Viet Nam, but most of them died the regular way like civilians do. That they're gone, pains me, but again, what I will write about is pain that hurts physically.

As far as I know, I'm one of the few of my army OCS class who doesn't live with some sort of extreme pain. Every year and a half, we have a reunion—in 2012 in St. Augustine, Florida, and March 2014 in San Diego, probably because the guy sponsoring it lives in California. Of those of us still around, only about eight made it to San Diego. Many of the guys live in pain from war wounds, but most of them do so from stuff that will happen to ordinary people like you and your friends when you become old farts someday (I won't give you a reason for the old fart terminology—if you dance at old folks homes, you know why I use it).

The guy I spent most of my time with in San Diego had been an athlete up until last year when he fell backwards and hit his head on something. As a result, he now walks like he's a hundred years old. When he talks, his speech is slurred, and he spits, so people don't want to stand in front of him.

I don't know what percentage of ordinary old folks have joint replacements, knees, ankles, or hips, but many of the still around guys I served with, have had one or two of them. Replacements are not the main reasons so few of them come to our reunions. Those who had them, make it. It's those with health problems which haven't been fixed, that don't make the reunions. Either that or the reason is that they or their wives are old.

The rest of this chapter is not dedicated to the pains that plague old people or the treatments that ease those pains. It's about those I've known personally. Perhaps I've been lucky or maybe because of the way I've maintained my health, I've had no replacements of parts. Maybe this chapter is out of place. Possibly it should have been included in a chapter about an unhealthy body being better than no body at all. Who knows? My body isn't as healthy as it was before I had a stroke over a year ago. Until a blood vessel burst on the right side of my brain, I had no extreme pains, just things that had to be fixed or that took care of themselves.

About ten years ago, twelve of us met at a reunion on a cruise ship out of a port in Texas. I had a limp, as did some of the others, but decided I was going to show the other guys, who were also in their late seventies, what great shape I was in. So every morning, for about a half-hour I walked around a topside deck, which was evidently built to be out of sight as none of the other guys saw me—at least they never joined me. Later, as we walked up steps to the dining room, I found I could hop up the steps, using calf muscles or other muscles close by, and it didn't require me to limp. I noticed that I was one of the few non-limpers on the stairs (*the ladder* in navy terminology). That's also how I found out about getting rid of the nicotine stains in my shorts. I'll tell about that later in the chapter if it doesn't still bother me to write about it by then.

By the last day of the eight day cruise around the Caribbean, I no longer limped, so I kept the same rigmarole up, walking each day. I figured I must have happened onto a solution for the problem; when I arrived home—the limp was gone. I don't know the cause and effect, and I don't know if it was the proper thing to do, but I decided I could handle similar future problems without surgery. At home I decided to walk two miles a day. I didn't want to freeze my buns in the Michigan winter, so I laid out a route in the house: Down the hall, through the bedroom and bath, back up the hall, around the pool table, through the living room, and the dining room, and back to the hall. I checked it out and found I could do two miles in forty minutes, so that became my regular morning routine.

I confess that part of the reason I decided to continue long walks each morning had nothing to do with being healthy or not having pain. When I was seventeen a couple of years ago, one day I watched as my mother sorted some of my dad's clothing in preparation to wash clothes. A pair of his white under shorts fell to the floor. Mom noticed I was looking at the brown stains on the rear of the shorts and she casually said, "Nicotine stains." I've remembered that for seventy years.

While walking on the cruise liner deck each morning, I found it solved the problem of my having nicotine stains, so after coming home, I began my two-mile walks after having a bowel movement. After the walk I wiped again, and from then on, the stains were no more. I don't know if this story about nicotine will ever bring tarnish to your life (or remove it), but it worked for me. But then, I was saddled with the need to do a long walk every morning.

I solved a newfound regularity problem by performing two simple tasks, neither one difficult to do: I eat a high fiber oat and chocolate bar for dessert after lunch and dinner, which each give me thirty-five percent of my daily fiber requirement—those along with a high fiber cereal each morning, fulfill my total fiber needs without having to worry about getting fiber the rest of the day. Then all I have to do is think about pooping for five or ten minutes, as I walk, and it doesn't even have to be for a mile (I don't poop as I walk—I just think about doing it).

During my morning walks, one day my left foot started hurting, so I changed my route to favor that foot, but it didn't help. I thought, to *hell with that foot,* and went back to my regular route, but slower. After a short time, the foot stopped hurting, and I resumed my faster speed. A couple of years later, I cut my morning walk to one mile simply because I was getting lazier, and occasionally I'd get a pain in a knee or a foot. I kept walking but ignored the pain and cussed at the foot or knee, favoring it for a bit. The pain disappeared, but I don't recommend that you use this method of relieving pain. You can try it if you feel inclined, but I'd recommend you do as the TV ads tell people: Check with your doctor.

I still had a new pain somewhere in my hip, that didn't seem to want to disappear (the pain—not the hip), but I couldn't tell exactly where the soreness was. It seemed to be somewhere deep. I ignored it and decided to tell my doctor about it, but before I got his opinion, as if by magic, it disappeared. Again, I don't recommend you ignore pain—instead see what your doctor says. This is a book, not a gospel, a book where I tell you what's happened to me as I've grown old, and what I've done about it. This entire story is how I've grown old ungracefully. It's not a recommendation for you to follow in my footsteps. I've talked to my doctor after I made various changes, and he's invariably shrugged and said, "You'll find out if it's what you should do." He was right. I've found out that what I've done is what I should keep doing. You can do whatever keeps you going the direction you want.

I get pains when I eat, from biting my tongue, cheek, or lip, and I know I'm not alone—other old people tell me they do it, too. I have arthritis in my neck, my wrists, and perhaps that's what causes the pain in my foot when I occasionally hobble during my morning walk, a pain I just ignore, and usually forget about. Another pain, that is always present and easy to remember, is when I bend over while dressing or to pick something off the floor, which often consists of something I dropped while dressing. I won't say any more about that problem. I already told you what my neighbor, John, said about not stooping to retrieve anything from the floor till he needs to get at least two things. Until I solved the problem, not only did stooping cause pain, but getting up after sitting reminded me in a hurry that I was getting old, or at least headed in that direction. In order to head off pain in the future, I practice bending over to touch my toes on a regular basis. Of course it may take a bit of time before I make it all the way to the toes.

Some aches, pains, or other uncomfortable feelings come with aging. Poor circulation still causes my hands and feet to be cold, along with other parts of my body, and it has got worse since I had a stroke. It gets even worse when I play gin rummy with Rosie at her house because she keeps the heat turned down lower than I do mine. Sometimes a strange pain may pop up, without apparent cause, in just about any part of my body.

I was walking down the hall last week when a sharp pain in my left foot caused me to falter, dropping me to my knees. Fortunately, my fall was broken when I reached out to the wall, and soon the pain disappeared. I figured it was because of the stroke and just compensated for it for a while.

Another problem I've become familiar with is tenderness through my entire body. When I bang an elbow or arm on a part of the house, such as a doorframe, it causes a pain in the muscle I banged. If I hold onto something too tight, such as a cup handle, or while carrying a clothes basket with more firmness than usual, my fingers will experience pain, causing me to drop it.

Most of the pains I've developed due to age, don't bother me that much. Perhaps I'll die of old age without ever having surgery. I have only a few problems with pain other than those caused by my stroke. I work on rehab, which is exercise, and do so without pain medication. My doctor agrees with my decision to avoid painkillers.

Growing Old Ungracefully / Phil Kline

If I did ask for a prescription, I think he'd say, "You probably won't live long enough to make it worth your while."

Growing Old Ungracefully / Phil Kline

EIGHT

THE LEARNING CURVE BALL

At age fifty-five, I started taking piano lessons at Lansing Community College, taking them each week and practicing an hour every day, loving it. I eventually got to the point in my second book of lessons where I could play simple tunes for my own enjoyment or to impress others with my newfound skill. I expected to continue, but it didn't happen. After thirty years of selling and training salespeople, I began teaching Sales at LCC. Because of the time spent doing so, I didn't have the time to continue my exercise program or practice what I'd learned to play.

The only texts on sales, available through publishing houses, were those written by college professors who had never sold a thing, so I complained to the Business Department dean about not having a text written by someone who'd been in real sales. He said, "Write your own."

I had never written before but, at about sixty, it was time. I wrote, keeping ahead of the class during the fall semester and putting it in draft form in the spring. After learning the ropes on how to get my text published, I accomplished it. So don't think you will reach a point where you can't change your life. I didn't think I could until I was forced to do so.

When I quit teaching two years ago, I decided to resume my piano lessons but found I had to go back almost to the start, and learn the basics again. Not only had I forgot what I'd learned, but I had grown old enough that learning to play piano wasn't fun anymore—it had become work. Learning anything is no longer as easy or exciting as it had been. Since I'd learned enough about writing to have been published I ditched the piano lessons and kept writing.

I was talking to Esther, a good friend of mine, who lives in Kansas. She said, "I hate having to learn new ways of doing things. I like the old ways I've done them for years. When my five year old computer crashed, I had an engineer transfer important stuff to the new one and some of what he supposedly transferred didn't work." I had the same type of problem Esther did, but instead of what she went through, my problem was when I bought a new I-Mac like my five year-old one. Doing so, I found that my Brother printer wouldn't work with the new I-Mac. Instead of contacting Brother myself, I had Rosie do it for me. I didn't want to contact Brother about my problem because I probably wouldn't understand what they told me. She got it to work.

I'm not a gadget nerd. I use the computer for word-processing, email, and for the simple functions I did ten, fifteen, or twenty years ago. I'm not turned on by new electronic gadgets. When I-phones came out, I was not excited about getting one—I didn't even want to learn how to use one. I finally got a cell phone at age eighty-six, only to take in my car in case of an emergency, or when I leave the house for an extended period. Learning used to be exciting for me. It ain't no more. I've had the cell phone for a year, but have only made one call on it to see if it worked. I haven't taken a photograph with it and probably never will.

Old age has taken away the excitement I used to have to learn how to use new gadgets. I'd never realized the extent to which learning disappeared as old age appeared. That itself wasn't a major problem until I decided to learn more about the effect aging was having on me, and what I could look forward to as I continued to grow even older. The major lesson I've learned is that even if I can no longer learn, at least I can write what I learned as I became an old fart.

A strange sideline to all this is that even in my dreams, I don't have the ability to learn, or to understand directions like I used to. I have dreams, and in them, almost without exception, I'm faced with a misunderstanding of directions or inability to understand something in the dream. When I awake, I find I'm still trying to solve the problem I dreamed about. You think it won't happen to you. It'll probably sneak up on you as it has with me. The stories I tell are intended to let you know there's the possibility that someday learning won't be as easy or as much fun as it used to be. Before it's too late, take heed if you want to learn something. Do it now.

I've watched a friend digress over the last twenty years. He flew as a crewmember of a B-17 Flying Fortress during World War II. As a member of the American Legion, he used to be active in conversations at meetings, but lately, he just attends, and doesn't become involved in subjects being tossed around. A change I've seen in him is that his voice has got so soft it's hard to understand what he says. Lately I've noticed a change in my voice, which seems to be headed in the same direction as his. He's a few years older than I am. When meetings are over, he is picked up by his wife in her car. Someday I may be in the same situation except I have no wife.

Not everything that happens with old age is untreatable. Even arthritis has a medication to reduce the pain or other negative effects. I don't use pain-relievers due to my high pain tolerance. I've mentioned having fingernails which split and toenails that curl up—I do something to prevent their negative effects. I used to think an emery board was made for women to shape their nails and make them prettier. Perhaps that's true, but I use one to prevent snagging of my clothes by a jagged fingernail. Toenails don't snag my pants or shirt, but at times get caught when I'm putting on a sock. It's hard enough reaching to put socks on without fighting obnoxious toenails. I clip and file them down till they're friendly. Just lately, I've discovered that I can't reach the toenails on one of my feet (I forget which one), so I'm making a concession and will have a personal pedicurist. I could eliminate that by having a wife, but a pedicurist is the lesser evil.

I don't listen as well as I used to. It used to be, when people told me their names, I'd remember them. Last year when a guy moved into the neighborhood, I walked to his home, extended my hand and told him my name was Phil Kline. He shook my hand and said his name was Paul something. I forgot his last name, evidently because it wasn't important enough for me to listen. That is something that happened when I reached a certain age. I forgot which age.

Two aspects in the process of remembering names have to be changed in my old age. First, I have to work on remembering names; it seems that each time someone gives me his or her name, I don't listen. Even if I do listen, I still have to make sure I do aspect number two: I have to come up with an association in order to remember the name.

I don't remember the date I'm supposed to see my doctor for a regular checkup or to see how he's doing, probably because it comes only once or twice a year. When I do see him, he checks me out and ensures I have a prescription to keep my blood pressure in tolerance, and asks if my gonorrhea has been acting up.

I compensate for my lack of memory about when to see him and other appointments by putting the information on the white-board next to my desk.

While again writing about remembering (or not remembering), one small detail jumps out that hasn't caused a problem for me yet, but is liable to someday. When I look at a clock to see what time it is, I sometimes read the time incorrectly by five or ten minutes. If it is five twenty-five, I may see it as being five twenty. It's probably happened to me half a dozen times this last month. Obviously the solution is to be more attentive and to concentrate on doing it right, the same as I concentrate on using a banister when I go up or down stairs.

A big problem I have in this old state (the state of being old, not the State of Michigan), is realizing that old age won't only cause my looks to change. I've already had a change of looks, and I expect I'll endure many more as I continue to age, unless that voice comes from above to send me back to age fifteen, as I expect it will. Maybe it'll happen to Rosie, too, so I won't have to dance with an old woman.

I've had a good life, and I still have exciting things I expect to do, so old age ain't all bad. So far I've found nothing that will keep me from living a pretty good life as an old fart. I just have to remember to dance slowly, so people will know I can still dance. If people suspect I'm doing so just to confuse them, I can always point to Rosie—behind her back, of course.

If you wish to learn how to slow down the aging process, read the next Chapter.

NINE

PRETEND

When you're young, if you have a problem, you go to a doctor to get fixed or wait it out until it fixes itself. But when you get old and have a problem, it usually won't go away—either get used to it or pretend it will go away. Do the things you did when you were young, and people will remark at how young you seem. You won't reduce your age, but many times you'll solve a problem that otherwise will linger. TV ads hawk facelifts and other products to make you seem younger. I'm not talking about what you can buy to impress others—I'm talking about what you can do to impress yourself with how young you feel. One of the best ways to do so is to pretend. Otherwise, you may as well accept the idea that you're too old to feel young again.

As I aged, I didn't fall other than when walking on snow except for the times when I'd been sitting and wanted to stand. I have fewer problems now because I pretend. Because I pretend that I won't fall back into the chair, I don't. I tell myself over and over that I'm going to overcome many problems this way. Suddenly I don't worry about them. What my neighbor, John, says about not picking up just one thing, is not true.

When I was young, I could bend far enough to touch my toes with my fingers, but after hearing John tell me that it was difficult for older people to bend, it began to happen to me—the problem wasn't my age. It was because I believed what John said.

I've decided I don't have to accept the problems people encounter with old age—perhaps some of them but not all. That concept was proved when I decided to pretend I was still young.

A year ago, before even thinking about this chapter, I had a stroke. While lying in a hospital bed for eleven days, I remembered two people I knew who had strokes at a younger age than I was when I had mine. One of them lived two houses down from me. I visited him, and all the while I was there, he cried. The woman who was his wife, now his widow, told me that all he did was feel sorry for himself and cry. He wasted away in bed. Just about everyone in the neighborhood agrees that he had no choice to have or not have the stroke, but his not recuperating from it was something he could have prevented.

The other friend who had a stroke about the same time was Dex, a college president, who had his while water skiing. Fortunately, one of the guys in the boat pulling him was a husky football player, and the other was a doctor. They pulled him out of the water and got him to a hospital. A few days later, I went to visit him and watched as he moved the fingers of one hand while tears rolled down his cheeks. "This is the first day I've been able to move anything on my left side," he said. "The doctor said I'd never walk without a cane. I told them I would never use a cane." A year later, Dex was on the job at the college, not using a cane. He never has used one, and I couldn't tell he'd had a stroke. His almost total recuperation was due to his positive attitude.

Two other stroke victims were in the room at Sparrow Hospital when I joined them there. To me, they seemed resigned to their fate. I wasn't. I felt, *If Dex could do it, I can too.* Nine days later, after taking daily rehab sessions, when I left the hospital to take care of myself, the other two stroke victims were still in the room, spending most of their days in bed. One important lesson I learned at rehab is: If you have a stroke, get to the emergency room right away.

After a month at Capitol Rehabilitation, a great outpatient rehab center, I continued my rehab at home, using what they had taught me. In addition, I pretended I could do things I had done before I had my stroke. I mowed my one-third acre lawn, raked leaves, and took care of the house alone. When the snowiest winter in the last fifty years came along, I shoveled the driveway at least seven times, including one snowfall of fifteen inches and at least two more of at least six inches. And I walk similar to the way I did before the stroke, when I remember to do so.

A woman from down the street stopped her car while I was in the yard picking up branches broken off by a storm. "You shouldn't be doing that," she said. I didn't tell her I was only pretending I was able to do it, or that later I'd pretend I could saw them up with a handsaw and burn them in the fireplace. And I didn't tell her that later I'd pretend to use an ax to split logs.

Pretending I can do things I used to be able to do is rewarding. I escape the feeling of being too old to do them. Years ago, I was able to reach down and touch my toes with ease. One year ago, I couldn't. Now I can reach them. I'm able to do so because I pretend I can.

I've reduced my clumsiness by pretending I'm not clumsy. I now carry things without the fear of dropping them because I'm practicing being normal, similar to rehab. By doing so, I've mostly eliminated having to clean up liquids or broken glass I've dropped (just mostly).

Every day for a year I've walked the way my rehab specialist, Andy, told me to do, by lifting my feet and digging my heels in while pretending to walk normally. I believe that because of doing what he said, I can and do walk at least a mile every day as soon as I finish hand exercises that have strengthened my left hand to a degree where I can use it in doing normal tasks necessary to live alone.

Like Dex, I don't use a cane—and I got my driver's license back. I perform many of the same jobs I would be doing if I hadn't had a stroke because I pretend I can do them.

It works.

Many old people have long plastic pillboxes with a row of little spaces, which have the days of the week written on them, a reminder to take drugs. At eighty-seven, I take one pill in the morning and one at night. Perhaps it's wrong for me to take so few, but I have two friends who sell pharmaceutical drugs and they both state that some of their physician clients are more interested in prescribing drugs than they should be. Take what your doctor recommends. I'm just writing about what I do.

I spent four days last month in San Diego with my army buddies on the 65th anniversary of our becoming second lieutenants. Of those of us left from the original graduates, who made the reunion, none of them—or their wives—were in great health yet they still enjoy life. Getting old doesn't mean the end of having a good time.

I'm a guy who believes he's had a great life and is concerned about living the way I want. If growing old bothers you, there may be something you can do about it. Pretending you're not old will help if you follow up that pretense by maintaining a positive attitude. But pretend to make changes only in those areas that are safe for you, and don't go telling others what you're doing—they may laugh at you. We don't have to worry about what people think of us. Those who give up are the ones who grow old and waste away.

I met a woman in her thirties who may just as well have been old. She had just finished her Ph.D. at the University of Michigan and was complaining that there were not as many jobs for a Ph.D. as there used to be, and she would have to take a job for which she was overqualified. I don't think her problem is that she's overqualified. Not many of today's jobs require an advanced degree, other than in colleges. The reason I mention her here is that she's stuck on the "used to be", the same as many old people are. Life is different now, so change to fit what is today.

I learned a lot about being able to overcome, from a woman I respect as much as I respect anyone. When she was twenty years old, she awoke one morning paralyzed in a fetal position with nobody around to take care of her. She's had problems other than the rheumatoid arthritis, which caused the paralysis. She has undergone multiple ankle, knee, hip, and shoulder replacements. Once when I had lunch with her, both of her arms were broken and in slings. In order to eat she took one arm out of the sling.

This woman went to college in a wheelchair and continued on to get her doctorate. She is now employed full-time as a professional. She writes on how to overcome adversity, and gives her books to people who can learn from them instead of trying to make money by selling them. She helped me change the way I look at what's happened in my life and where I go from here. I hope what I've learned from her about improving my life, can do the same for you.

If you ever feel sorry for yourself for changes which affect you, remember the good things that have happened to you. Consider the wonderful life you've had, and what you have done to make the lives of others more satisfying. By pretending you're not old, you won't have to die with dignity to keep from growing old ungracefully.

Much of the time I feel like a Lazy-Good-For-Nothin'. I've mentioned this feeling to a couple of old friends, and they said, "Get used to it." Sometimes that feeling still triumphs, but most of the time, I pretend I'm doing what I'm supposed to do, and when I do so, the feeling is forgotten.

Yesterday I did two hours of rehab exercises, including walking a mile, and spent another hour following a lawnmower around, mowing my yard, all the time, pretending I could do it.

A wise person, who was not a friend, wrote a message I saw when I went to Jake's Plumbing Shop in Lansing, Michigan. I was heading to get a faucet for my kitchen sink and realized I was there when I saw a back yard covered with old toilets, sinks, and urinals. While waiting to get my faucet, I noticed a framed quote above a display case. I asked for a copy of it and was given one, which I framed. Jake is gone now, but his theory on living hangs near my kitchen sink: "Life's journey is not to arrive at the grave safely in a well preserved body, but rather to skid in sideways, totally worn out, shouting,'Holy shit—what a ride!!'"

Growing Old Ungracefully / Phil Kline

TEN

THE GOOD PART OF BEING OLD

Memories have provided me with advantages others may not gain because they're not old yet. You've probably never experienced getting out of school and heading to the candy store to buy a penny's worth of candy. That's what I used to do. I seldom had a nickel to buy a whole candy bar. And you may never have heard the song that goes: "If I had a nickel, I'll tell you what I'd do. I'd spend it all for candy and give it all to you," or know who said, "I vant to be alone."

I remember going downtown in Wollaston, Massachusetts to the 3 Cent Store, where everything in the store cost three cents—I bought a bamboo backscratcher there. Later in life, after inflation set in, I graduated to shopping at The Five and Ten Cent Store. My mother could buy anything she wanted from Johnson's Market for less than thirty dollars a month for our family of six. Many times I went with her to help carry bags of groceries, some of which she wasn't charged for. She didn't have to pay for items such as beef tongue, hearts, chicken wings, and many other chicken parts. It seemed as if Mr. Johnson gave us kids a bit of free candy or ice cream whenever we were with Mom. Back then there was no such thing as overweight kids.

Another memory I have, which you never experienced, is the time I crossed the Pacific Ocean with my young wife, dancing to songs of Dinah Shore and Bing Crosby, as played by the ship's band. We danced to every song, every night for two weeks and walked hand-in-hand in the sun of the upper deck during the day.

Memories extend to junior high school, singing songs with the entire class every day before studies began, to my first date in high school, and to the high I got when Michigan State College won the 1956 Rose Bowl game. Exceptional accomplishments got people high back then.

I'm thankful to have been born years ago. Otherwise I wouldn't have had the opportunity to ride cows on Grandfather's farm, to learn to milk while sitting on a one-legged stool, or to ride seven miles to town every Saturday in a Model T Ford, in order to sell the cream from a separator, on which I had sweated from turning the crank. We fed the leftover skim milk, mixed with bran, to the hogs. That's where I learned to call them with a loud, "Sooey, Sooey, Sooey."

Some days are worse than others, but I have to remind myself occasionally that some are better, too. You can do the same the next time you have a bad one.

THE END, at last.

ABOUT THE AUTHOR

Phil Kline has been a salesman and sales trainer most of his adult life. Shortly after he was hired to teach sales at the Community College of Lansing, Michigan, he began looking for books on the subject. He soon came to realize the only ones on the market were academic, written by professors who had never made a sale in their life. When he complained, the dean suggested Phil write such a book himself. In much the same way—and driven by the same frustration of finding nothing on the market that would adequately prepare one for advancing years--Phil wrote *Growing Old Ungracefully*. When he isn't sharing the truth about sales and aging, Phil is a successful playwright and community leader.

Made in the USA
Middletown, DE
17 February 2015